What readers are saying about In 30 Minutes® guides:

Google Drive & Docs In 30 Minutes

"I bought your Google Docs guide myself (my new company uses it) and it was really handy. I loved it."

"I have been impressed by the writing style and how easy it was to get very familiar and start leveraging Google Docs. I can't wait for more titles. Nice job!"

Genealogy Basics In 30 Minutes

"This basic genealogy book is a fast, informative read that will get you on your way if you are ready to begin your genealogy journey or are looking for tips to push past a problem area."

"The personal one-on-one feel and the obvious dedication it took to boil down a lot of research into such a small book and still make it readable are the two reasons I give this book such a high rating. Recommended."

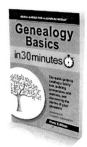

Twitter In 30 Minutes

"A perfect introduction to Twitter. Quick and easy read with lots of photos. I finally understand the # symbol!"

"Clarified any issues and concerns I had and listed some excellent precautions."

D0962922

LinkedIn In 30 Minutes

"This book does everything it claim.. to LinkedIn and gives you tips on how to make a good profile."

"I already had a LinkedIn account, which I use on a regular basis, but still found the book very helpful. The author gave examples and explained why it is important to detail and promote your account."

Excel Basics In 30 Minutes

"Fast and easy. The material presented is very basic but it is also accessible with step-by-step screenshots and a friendly tone more like a friend or co-worker explaining how to use Excel than a technical manual."

"An excellent little guide. For those who already know their way around Excel, it'll be a good refresher course. Definitely plan on passing it around the office."

Learn more about In 30 Minutes® guides at in30minutes.com

Microsoft Word

In 30 Minutes

How to make a bigger impact
with your documents and master
Word's writing, formatting, and
collaboration tools

Angela Rose

Microsoft Word In 30 Minutes
ISBN: 978-1-939924-70-4
Library of Congress Control Number: 2016954365
Copyright © 2016 by i30 Media Corporation.

Cover and interior design *by* Monica Thomas for TLC Graphics, www.TLCGraphics.com. Interior design and composition assisted *by* Rick Soldin, book-comp.com.

Contents

Contents

Contents

Contents

Contents

Introduction

In 1985 I experienced my first broken bone.

I didn't shatter a femur skydiving, or have my rib cracked by an anaconda. Nor did the accident involve any other brave undertaking, natural disaster, or wild animal. Instead, my proximal phalanx (otherwise known as my big toe) was broken by a humble typewriter. An off-white, manual, portable typewriter from Sears, to be precise.

I had received the typewriter as a 12th birthday gift the year before, fancying myself the next great American novelist. I had a lot of fun with that typewriter, composing tales of adolescent highs and lows and attempting to emulate the storytelling styles of Erma Bombeck and Judy Bloom—my favorite authors at the time. Then I dropped the typewriter. On my foot. And it broke my big toe.

I never felt the same about typewriters after that. In fact, since adopting a personal computer complete with word processing software as my writing tool of choice more than two decades ago, I had forgotten about the typewriter. Now the most distressing inconvenience I encounter while plying my trade is my feline assistants jumping on the keyboard. But thanks to Microsoft Word, I can erase the random gibberish they insert into my documents with a quick tap of the backspace key rather than using up hours with painstaking, manual corrections.

Word also allows me to add photos, make tables and charts, and change font styles, sizes and colors with a few clicks. Checking spelling and grammar is instantaneous, and finding alternate words using the built-in thesaurus is a breeze. I can even save my documents to the cloud so others can share their comments.

Given all that, I can honestly say Microsoft Word is fahskath[b?ti[ghoiga;bs kjht[g'hhslgg'hl!

More than just a word processor

Millions of people use Microsoft Word every day. I cannot imagine working as a freelance writer without it—the program is essential to my work writing magazine articles, blog posts, website text, and even books like the one you are reading right now. But you don't have to make your living stringing words together to benefit from Microsoft Word. Almost anyone will find dozens of personal and professional uses for this versatile program.

What are people doing with Microsoft Word? Here are just a few examples:

➤ **Eve just graduated from high school and is heading off to college.** She has used Word in the past for term papers, but plans to use it a lot more this fall. From typing up lecture notes to organizing her study schedule and homework deadlines, Eve will rely on Word documents to keep her goals on track. Further, uploading files to OneDrive will allow her to access them from her PC at home, her laptop in the classroom, or even her phone when she is on the go.

➤ **Phil uses Microsoft Word every day, and has been doing so since the 1990s.** However, he's avoided upgrading until now because he doesn't want to have to relearn how to use it. He bought this book because he's worried about all the new features and wants to get up to speed on the user interface for Word 2016 as quickly as possible.

➤ **Robert has never used a word processor before.** His career as a metalworker never required it. Now he has retired and wants to record his family's history. He is slowly learning to type and plans to use Word to create documents containing his family tree, stories he heard from his grandparents, and photos of various ancestors that he has collected over the years. Once he has created a document that contains all of the text and images, Word will make it easy for him to format, print, and distribute it to relatives all over the country.

➤ **Shahida is preparing to search for a new job.** She has used Word numerous times in her current position as an office manager, but she is excited about creating an eye-catching résumé and cover letter based on the new templates in Word 2016.

➤ **Annie is writing her first book about the care and training of cats.** She is going to use Word 2016 for her Windows PC as well as Word Online to prepare her manuscript. Once she has a draft in hand, she will turn to friends and family who have offered help as proofreaders. Word's Track Changes feature will make it easy to accept or reject their suggestions.

➤ **Fernando recently subscribed to Office 365 in preparation for launching a new company.** He is currently using Word to put together a business plan complete with tables, charts and footnoted research that should impress prospective investors. Fernando will use Word's security features to ensure that only selected people will be able to review the business plan.

I have written this guide—complete with step-by-step instructions, screen-shots, and plenty of cat-related anecdotes—to help all kinds of people quickly learn basic features and tools of Word 2016. It is not a compre-hensive guide, and certain advanced topics are excluded. Nevertheless, *Microsoft Word In 30 Minutes* covers all of the basics as well as most inter-mediate-level topics, including:

➤ Navigating Word's Ribbon.

➤ How to create a new document.

➤ Formatting, styles, and themes.

➤ How to save, print, and export Word files.

➤ Easy ways to add cool elements such as images and charts.

➤ How to whip up a table of contents, indexes, and footnotes.

➤ How to make sure your copy is perfect.

➤ Collaboration and other ways to share documents.

Even better, you will learn all of this in about 30 short minutes. That is less time than most of us spend watching funny cat videos (or dog videos, if you're not into cats) on YouTube every day! We don't have any time to lose, so let's get started.

CHAPTER 1

Interface basics

My cats are creatures of habit. They have favorite napping spots and rotate through them at approximately the same time every day. They prefer to eat their meals out of their favorite bowls and in their usual spots on the main floor of our home at 8 a.m. and 6 p.m. each day. They are also happiest with a limited menu, and rarely enjoy other options. Present them with a new flavor of cat food or (heaven forbid!) a smorgasbord of leftover cans, and it is enough to frazzle their kitty minds.

When it comes to my writing routines, I am a lot like my cats. Distraction is my enemy. Choices—who needs 'em? And when it comes to change, let's just say I look forward to switching up my writing routines just about as much as my cats look forward to a crusty can of leftovers. So I was not too thrilled about upgrading to Word 2016, and delayed it as long as I could. But once I gave it a spin, I discovered I had nothing to fear—and neither should you! Here's why:

➤ **The interface has not changed a lot.** If you are like me and you are migrating from Word 2013 or Word 2010, then Word 2016 (and Word Online) will seem quite familiar.

➤ **The newest version of Word has a number of really cool features** that have made my work more efficient. They include improved online storage, easy-to-use collaboration, and a swanky new *Tell Me* tool.

➤ Even if you are new to Microsoft Word (or haven't used it in a long time) **the interface is super intuitive and a snap to learn**—especially with *Microsoft Word In 30 Minutes* by your side!

The different flavors of Microsoft Word

This edition of *Microsoft Word In 30 Minutes* was written primarily for the desktop version of the software for both Windows and Mac. However, you may also find it useful if you want to use Word Online, an online version of Word accessed through a Web browser. There are also several Word mobile apps, which are mentioned below, but they are outside of the scope of this edition.

There are two main differences between the desktop version of Microsoft Word and Word Online: cost and functionality.

Word 2016 vs. Word Online: Cost

As of this writing, it is still possible to purchase the full version of Word 2016 (to install on a single PC) for about $110. Word 2016 is also part of the Microsoft Office 2016 software suite, which costs about $230.

However, these options may not be available much longer. In recent years, Microsoft has been pushing customers to subscribe to Word and other programs in the Office family. You can subscribe to Office 365 Home for $10 per month and get Word, Excel, PowerPoint, OneNote, and Publisher for up to five PCs, five tablets, and five phones.

I found the Office 365 subscription to be the best deal. Not only can you share unused installations with friends and family members, but the software suite will also automatically update whenever a new version is released, for as long as you maintain your subscription.

To start a subscription, visit office.microsoft.com and select Office 365. You will need to register for a Microsoft account, activate the subscription, and download and install the entire office suite, which includes the most recent version of Microsoft Word. It is possible to turn off the subscription if you do not anticipate using it for a few months, and then reactivate it later.

Word Online, on the other hand, is totally free. That may sound wonderful, but "free" comes at a cost—in this case, reduced functionality.

Protip: You already have a Microsoft account if you use Xbox Live, Skype, Hotmail, or practically any other Microsoft-owned service that requires registration. You can use the same login credentials to start an Office 365 subscription or use Word Online, or you can create a new Microsoft account.

Word 2016 vs. Word Online: Functionality

Word 2016 is a powerhouse, developed and improved over several decades. As you will learn over the chapters that follow, the features are extensive and can help you create documents that look amazing. For example, here is the selection of tools available on the Insert tab of Word 2016:

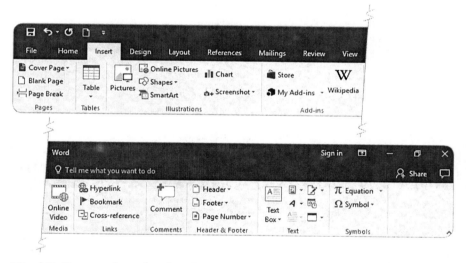

Word Online, on the other hand, is a stripped-down version of the software that is just a few years old. It opens up in a Web browser, but it contains far fewer formatting and design tools. You can see a much reduced set of features on the Insert tab in Word Online:

While most of the tools work the same way, you will basically be limited to simple word processing tasks—composing a new document, applying basic formatting, and simple collaboration.

In addition, you can only use Word Online when you have Internet access. This means you cannot use Word Online to write the next Great American Novel while riding a bus across the country or camping in the middle of the wilderness. You also cannot use Word Online in a coffee shop, airport lounge, hotel room, or home unless you can connect to the Internet.

If you want to try Word Online, go to office.com, select Word Online, and log in or register using a Microsoft account.

Mobile apps for Android and iOS

Word apps for Android and iOS devices have an impressive feature set, but are limited by the small screen size, a lack of a real keyboard, and issues associated with saving local files. The apps allow for common formatting tasks such as changing fonts and colors and adding bulleted lists, but can also handle more sophisticated options—from inserting tables to tracking changes.

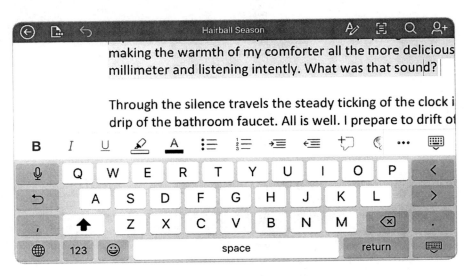

The apps are available for free on Google Play (Android phones and tablets) and the App Store (iOS devices such as the iPhone and iPad). However, the free app will only let you view Word documents—an Office 365 subscription is required to create or edit documents on your mobile device. You will also need a Bluetooth keyboard if you plan on doing any serious writing or editing.

While you will get increased app functionality if you purchase an Office 365 subscription, you are still going to need to use Word 2016 on a desktop or laptop if you want to maximize your formatting and design options.

In the chapters that follow, I will mostly refer to the desktop version of Microsoft Word for Windows PCs and macOS (formerly known as Mac OS X) as well as certain features that are available in Word Online.

OneDrive

With Word 2016, Microsoft has increased integration with OneDrive, the company's cloud storage service that was formerly branded as SkyDrive. The service is free to use with a Microsoft account, although greater amounts of storage will be allocated to Office 365 subscribers and business users.

Files saved to OneDrive are stored in remote server farms operated by Microsoft. There are several advantages associated with saving a file to OneDrive:

➤ Documents can be accessed from any logged-in PC or mobile device.

➤ Even if your computer breaks or gets stolen, documents on OneDrive can still be opened using another computer or device.

➤ OneDrive enables special sharing and collaboration options, including the ability to simultaneously collaborate on the same document.

However, there are some drawbacks to OneDrive. Most importantly, the service requires Wi-Fi or a network connection to sync files or activate collaboration options. In addition, OneDrive's syncing and cross-platform abilities are not as slick as Dropbox and other cloud storage services.

Launching Word

To get started with Word 2016, click the Word 2016 icon on your desktop, dock, or in your applications folder. To launch Word Online, go to office.com and select *Word Online*. You may need to log in with your Microsoft account credentials.

The first thing that appears after the program launches is the *Start Screen* (Windows and Word Online) or *Backstage View* (macOS). The Start Screen is divided into a list of recent documents (the left third of the screen) and the new document gallery (the right two-thirds of the screen).

From the Start Screen, you can take the following actions:

> ➤ **Open an existing document.** If you want to resume work on an old document, you can look for it in the list of recent documents on the left side of the window. Within this list, Word 2016 includes documents you've worked on in recent days and weeks, making it easy to get back to current projects. Simply click on the document you want to access or, if it is not listed, choose *Open other documents* at the bottom of the list (Windows) or *Open in OneDrive* (Word Online). You can then

navigate to the document's location on your computer or on OneDrive if you have saved it to Microsoft's cloud.

➤ **Open a blank document.** If you want to start a fresh document totally from scratch, simply select the blank page thumbnail in the new document gallery.

➤ **Open a template.** Word 2016 includes hundreds of templates for virtually anything you might want to create for home or business use. These include business cards, plans and reports, invoices, brochures, postcards, newsletters, posters and flyers, invitations, letters, and résumés. Template thumbnails are displayed in the new document gallery. You can browse them by category or enter keywords into the search bar. Then just click the thumbnail to start a new document using your template of choice.

Protip: While Word 2016 can open .doc documents created with earlier versions of the software, you will need to convert them to .docx files in order to use some of Word 2016's newer features. Select *File* at the top left of your screen to access Word's Backstage View. Select *Info* from the menu on the left before clicking on *Compatibility Mode*. In some cases, conversion to .docx may result in minor formatting or layout changes.

It's possible to launch Word 2016 for Windows by opening an existing document from your hard drive, instead of clicking on the Word icon. However, you will not see Backstage View. You also won't see the Start Screen if you begin a new document while you are already working on an existing one. In either of these cases, you can get to the new document gallery through Word's Backstage View. Just select *File* (at the top of the screen) and then *New* (from the Backstage View menu on the left). To get to a previously created document, select *File* and then *Open* (Windows) or *Recent* from the Backstage View menu (macOS).

Word Online can only be launched from a browser, and can only open files stored in OneDrive. In other words, it is not possible to open a .docx file on your hard drive using Word Online. In addition, even if you are already using Word Online, you may be prompted to choose between editing a particular document in Word 2016 installed on your computer or editing it in the browser. Choose the *Browser* option to make edits in Word Online.

Backstage View

Word 2016's Backstage View screen is a one-stop shop for many common tasks, including starting new documents and saving files. The Windows version of Backstage View also includes additional features, such as exporting files, printing, and changing certain software settings.

You can get to Backstage View at any time by clicking on *File* (Windows or Word Online) or the File icon (macOS) located at the top left of your screen. Navigating Backstage View is easy, thanks to the simple menu displayed on the left side of the screen:

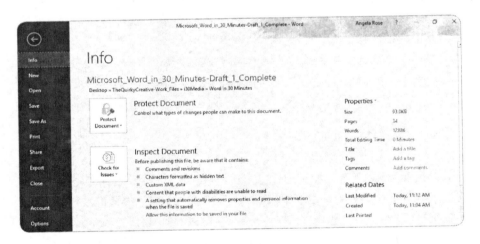

We will go into more detail on many of these menu items later in the book. For the time being, here's a quick overview of the tools in Backstage View for the Windows version of Word 2016:

> ➤ **Info.** Review your document's properties such as file size, page count, and word count. You can also access tools for protecting, inspecting,

and managing the document. We will dig deeper into the protection options in Chapter 5.

➤ **New.** Start a new document from scratch or select a template for customization.

➤ **Open.** Open an existing document stored on your computer, network, or the cloud.

➤ **Save and Save As.** Select one of these options to save your document under its current file name or save a copy in a new location, under a new file name or as a different file type. We will talk more about saving files in Chapter 2.

➤ **Print.** This is where you will go when it's time to print your Word document. We will dig deeper into printing in Chapter 2.

➤ **Share.** Word 2016 includes a number of collaboration features. You will learn the basics of sharing documents in Chapter 5.

➤ **Export.** Save a document as .doc or .docx, or create a PDF version. Export options will be explained in more detail in Chapter 2.

➤ **Close.** If you don't want to close your Word document using the "X" in the top-right corner of the document, you can click *Close* in Backstage View.

➤ **Account.** If you have purchased an Office 365 subscription, you can access your account settings and recent updates here.

➤ **Options.** Word 2016 includes plenty of settings you can customize to your liking. We will explore specific options later in the book.

To exit the Backstage View screen and return to your document, simply click on the back arrow at the top of the menu (Windows or Word Online) or click the *Cancel* button (macOS).

Backstage View for the Mac version of Word 2016 covers new file creation and opening existing documents, as well as access to basic account information. However, *Save As, Print, Share, Export,* and *Close* are not visible from the Mac version of Backstage View and have to be accessed via the *File* drop-down menu at the top of the screen. As for *Options*, many settings in the Mac version of Word 2016 can be accessed via *Word > Preferences*.

Backstage View in Word Online is similar to the full Windows version, but does not include *Options* or *Account*.

Navigating Word's Ribbon interface

If you have not used Word in the past decade or so, there will be a slight learning curve associated with Word's Ribbon interface, which first debuted in Word 2007 and is still used for Word 2016. The Ribbon contains basic features such as search, sharing, and an icon to save the document. But the real action takes place on eight primary tabs, each corresponding to a Ribbon-like strip of nifty tools.

We will start with a brief overview of what you will find on each tab before digging into specific explanations of some of the coolest and most useful features. Note that there are also several contextual tabs which are hidden from view until certain tools are activated. Several of these will be explained later in the book.

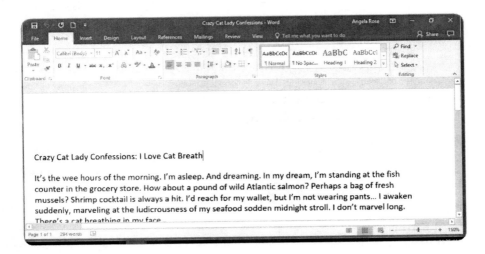

➤ **Home.** This is the default tab when you open or create a new document in Word. From here you can copy, paste, and cut text as well as access the clipboard. This is also where you will select fonts, change font sizes, add text effects and typography, create bulleted and numbered lists, format paragraphs, apply styles, and access several other editing features.

➤ **Insert.** Want to add some super-cool visual elements to your document? The tools you need probably live on this tab. They include buttons to create tables and insert pictures, charts, and media. You will also select this tab if you want to add cover pages, blank pages, hyperlinks, headers, and footers. Some of the tools, such as tables and pictures, come with their own contextual tabs as well.

➤ **Design.** Apply a predesigned theme (a collection of fonts, colors, and effects) to your document or create a theme of your very own. You can also customize the background of your page with colors, borders, and watermarks. I have rarely needed the tools on this tab, but you might if you are looking to add some pizzazz to a résumé, report, or brochure.

➤ **Layout.** Adjust page size, orientation, margins, and columns. Add page breaks and line numbers. You can even adjust hyphenation, indentation, and line spacing here as well as arrange layered elements on the page.

➤ **References.** Create a table of contents or index, add footnotes and endnotes, insert citations, and caption pictures. Again, this may not be a tab you regularly visit in your day-to-day use of Word, but the References tab is indispensable for research reports, term papers, and manuscripts.

➤ **Mailings.** This is where you will find the tools you need to create envelopes and mailing labels. The Mailings tab also handles mail merges, which involve importing addresses or a mailing list into a document or envelope template. These features are useful if you want to create, print, and mail marketing promotions, family newsletters, or other forms of bulk mail.

➤ **Review.** If you are a careful wordsmith, or work on a team, you will frequently access the Review tab. This is where you can access spelling and grammar tools, a thesaurus, tools to check the length of the document, and even a language translator. I use tools on this tab almost every time I work with a Word document, both to ensure I am producing quality copy and to incorporate edits my clients have suggested using comments and Word's *Track Changes* feature. The security features found on the Review tab will be discussed in more detail in Chapter 5.

➤ **View.** Whether you want to adjust your document's on-screen layout, work with the ruler or gridlines, access the navigation pane, zoom in or out, view multiple documents side-by-side or give the split screen a try, you will do it all here.

➤ **Contextual tabs.** Microsoft Word also has several hidden tabs that pop into view when you are working on certain tasks. For instance, when you insert a table into a document, two special contextual tabs will appear, containing tools to change the design and layout of the table. There are a number of contextual tabs, some of which will be covered in the chapters that follow.

Unlike previous releases of Microsoft Word, the Ribbon and tabs have nearly identical features on both the Windows and Mac versions of Word 2016. Where there are differences, I have attempted to explain them below.

However, the Word Online interface has a greatly simplified Ribbon and a limited set of features. There are no Design, References, or Mailings tabs in Word Online, and some of the tabs that are present have just a handful of features. I will try to note the missing features. Keep in mind that Microsoft updates Word Online with new tools from time to time, so even if a particular feature is missing from Word Online now, it may be introduced at some point in the future.

Other features of the Ribbon

In addition to the primary tabs described above, the Ribbon includes several additional features:

➤ **Tell Me.** New to the Windows version of Word 2016 and Word Online is the Tell Me feature. It's a small search field located above the

Ribbon's toolbar. Type in some text (for instance, "export file" or "set page margins") and Word will display a menu of helpful options. This can save you loads of time you would otherwise have spent scrolling through the Office Help Center. It's useful when you forget where to find a specific tool or you need to know which tool is necessary for a particular task.

➤ **Sharing options.** Also new to all versions of Microsoft Word is the ability to share your document with others. Look for the silhouette icon on the right side of the Ribbon to display sharing options, which include sharing via OneDrive (Microsoft's cloud storage service) or sending it as an email attachment. Chapter 5 describes sharing and collaboration in more detail.

➤ **Quick Access Toolbar.** At the very top left of the Ribbon (Windows only) is a small arrow that reveals the Quick Access Toolbar. You can customize it to include some of the tools you use most often by clicking on the little arrow to the right and checking the relevant tools. Mine is set up with the icons for Save, Undo Typing, and Repeat Typing. However, you can also add commands such as New, Open, Email, Quick Print, Print Preview and Print, Spelling and Grammar, Draw Table, and more.

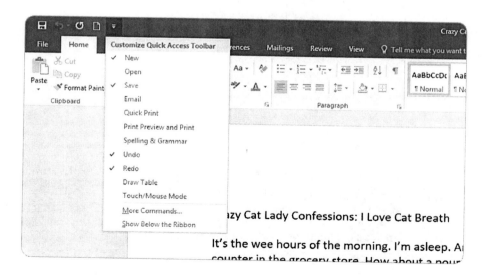

➤ **File name.** The document's file name is located at the top center of the Ribbon.

➤ **Your name.** If you are signed into your Microsoft account, your name will appear in the upper right of the Ribbon (Windows and Word Online; on a Mac the account info will be displayed in Backstage View).

➤ **Hiding the Ribbon.** Personally, I prefer to have the entire Ribbon—including the toolbars associated with the open tab—visible at the top of my screen when working in Word. Doing so helps me remember all the options I have for formatting text. However, it is possible to hide the Ribbon. Just click on the up-down arrow icon in the top right corner of your screen. The Windows version of Word 2016 includes a menu with the following options:

▷ Auto-hide Ribbon: no Ribbon.

▷ Show Tabs: Ribbon title tabs visible.

▷ Show Tabs and Commands: the entire Ribbon is visible at all times.

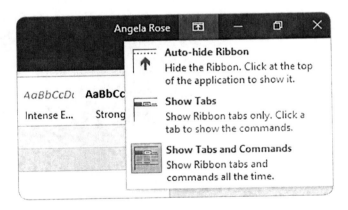

Protip: You can customize the Ribbon to better suit your needs and preferences. In the Windows version of Word 2016, select *File* at the top left of the screen to get to Backstage View, then *Options > Customize Ribbon*. On Macs, select the *Word* drop-down menu at the top of the screen, and then select *Preferences > General* to see the options under

Personalization. There are no Ribbon customization options for Word Online.

Display options for individual documents

Do you ever get tired of looking at the same old things in the same old ways, day in and day out? I sure do! Fortunately, we don't have to succumb to this boredom while using Word because Microsoft provides a variety of options for looking at documents using the View tab. Let's take a closer look at how to use some of these tools to change the ways in which Word files are displayed.

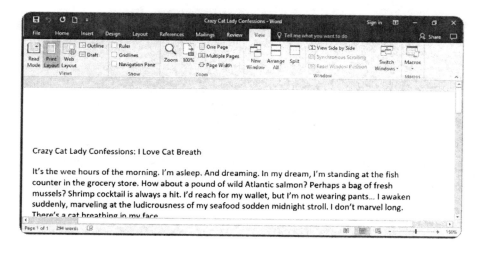

How to choose a view

On the left side of the View tab are a number of buttons to change the document view. If you are like me, you will get the most out of the following three options:

➤ **Print Layout.** This is Word's default view, and by far the one I use most often. It displays your document as a single, scrollable page.

➤ **Draft.** View your document without headers, footers, or marginalia such as comments and tracked changes. It's great for editing complex documents when you want to focus on the text.

➤ **Read Mode (Windows only).** If you are done writing and editing and want to review the text and other elements in your document without the distraction of ribbons, this is the view for you. It displays your document as an open book, with side-by-side pages and arrows for easy navigation.

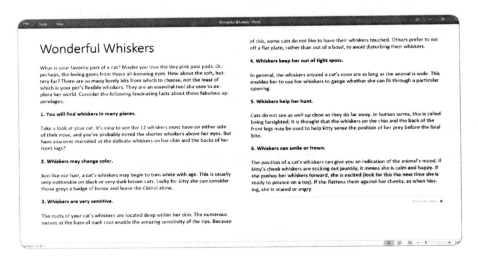

Word Online has only two view options on the View tab: *Editing View* and *Reading View*. Even though the two views are very basic, they are quite effective for basic editing and review.

How to display rulers and gridlines

There may be occasions in which you want to measure sections of your document, line up objects, or add an element to a particular location on a page. Simply check (or uncheck) the Ruler and Gridlines boxes on the View tab.

The ruler shows markers for the left and right margins, as well as markers for setting indentation and tabs. The following example shows a one-inch wide left margin, which is represented by the shaded part of the ruler. The stacked markers show the paragraph's left edge, which starts at less than 1/8 of an inch from the left margin with no indentation. There is also a tab marker located 2.5 inches from the left margin:

Sliding the markers along the ruler will change the settings on the screen and in the printed output, but only for highlighted text or the text containing the cursor. For this reason, it is better to change these settings for your entire document by modifying individual styles. This will be described in more detail in Chapter 3.

Word Online does not have settings for rulers or gridlines.

How to get your zoom on

Word provides several easy ways to enlarge or shrink the text on your documents. Use the *Zoom* options on the View tab to get started. I personally never use the *One Page* or *Multiple Page* options, as the resulting text is too tiny to read. However, click on *Page Width* and Word will zoom in (or out) until the width of the page matches the width of the window. If you prefer your text to appear a bit smaller, try clicking on 100%. If you want to manually adjust your zoom, select the magnifying glass. You can also do this by dragging the slider in the lower-right corner of the window (Windows and Mac) or clicking the percentage in the lower-right corner of the browser (Word Online).

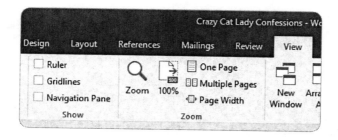

Note that changing the zoom percentage will only change how it looks on the screen—there will be no impact on the printed output. To change the size of text on the document itself, use the font size field or the formatting presets, which are all located on the Home tab.

How to work with multiple windows

On occasion, you may find that you want to work with two documents at once. Perhaps you want to refer to an outline while working on a draft, or you may need to work on two sections of the same document at the same time. To activate these features, check out the following tools in the View tab on Word 2016:

➤ **New Window.** This tool will open a second copy of your current document. Changes you make in either copy will be incorporated in the other as well.

➤ **Arrange All.** Once you have two copies of your document open, use this tool to stack them. This makes it easy to view different sections of the same document.

➤ **Split.** The document will be split into two stacked views, each with its own scrollbar. This is another way to view different sections of the same document.

➤ **View Side by Side.** When you are working with two different documents rather than two copies of the same document, this tool will arrange them side-by-side on your computer screen (Windows only).

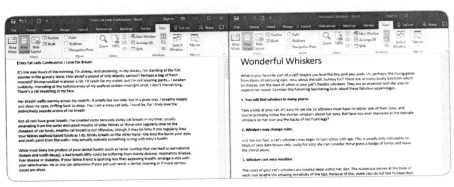

Note: These options are not available to users of Word Online.

CHAPTER 2

Creating, saving, and printing

By now you are starting to get a picture of the many things Word was built to do. You have enjoyed a brief overview of the dozens of tools you can use to design, format, and view documents.

However, you may still be worried that actually using the software will be difficult. Let me assure you it won't be. In fact, it's so easy, even a cat can use Word.

I am not joking. One of my three cats is Tegan the Floof, whose official title is Executive Interrupter. She loves to walk across my lap and plunk herself down on my computer keyboard, regardless of whether or not I am actively using it. One time I left my desk unattended to refresh my beverage. When I came back, this was on the screen:

It looks like Tegan was preparing to advertise a pool party, though I don't know why. She doesn't like water or socializing in group settings. Nevertheless, in a few short minutes, she'd managed to navigate to the new document gallery, select and download a template, and begin the customization process. If a cat can do it, so can you!

As mentioned in Chapter 1, the Start Screen and Backstage View offer access to prebuilt document templates in the new document gallery. They include dozens of invitations and flyers, including the Summer Event flyer shown above. It takes just a few clicks to see what is available and start adding your own text. In the next few pages, we will go over various options for saving and printing your work.

How to save a file

In Chapter 1, you learned how to open a Word file, create a new document based on a template or start a blank document from scratch. Once you have started working on a document, you are going to want to save the file as quickly and as often as you can. Take it from someone who has lost an important document in the past: You never know when a computer crash, power outage, or cat butt is going to strike.

Fortunately, saving your new Word file is easy. In Word Online, saving takes place automatically. In Word 2016, simply click the disk icon in the Quick Access Toolbar in the top left corner of the window. You can then name the file, select a format, and choose a location to store your document—typically OneDrive or a local hard drive.

After giving the file a name and a storage location, saving your progress will be nearly invisible. Use one of the following methods to regularly save an existing file:

➤ Click the disk icon.

➤ Select *File > Save.*

➤ Use a keyboard shortcut (Control-S for Windows, Command-S for Macs).

Protip: You can further protect yourself against lost documents by enabling auto recovery. If there is an unexpected system failure, you will be able to access the most recent version of the lost file. In Word 2016 for Windows, select *File > Options > Save* and then check the box next to *Save auto recover information*. In Word 2016 for Macs, select *Word > Preferences > Save* and check *Save Autorecover Info*.

How to duplicate a file

You may occasionally want to save multiple versions of a document or use an older document as the starting point for a new one. In either case, creating a duplicate is easy:

1. Open the file you want to duplicate.
2. Select *File > Save As.*
3. Enter a new file name.
4. Select the file type and the storage location.

Which file format should I use?

Word 2016 includes 19 different file formats to choose from. It's a safe bet you will never need the majority of them, which include HTML web pages and obscure XML formats. The ones you are most likely to use are:

➤ **Word Document (.docx).** This has been the default file format since the release of Word 2007. You can identify this file type by the extension .docx at the end of the file name. Save your files as this type unless you have a reason to use one of the types that follow.

➤ **Word 97-2003 Document (.doc).** There are still older versions of Microsoft Word in use. If someone you know is using a version of the software that is more than 10 years old, you will probably need to share a .doc version of the file with them. Note that while .doc files can be opened on newer versions of Word, certain features of Word 2016 may be incompatible with the older file format.

➤ **Word Template.** You have learned a little about the templates Microsoft has included with Word 2016, but did you know that you can also create your own? To save a document as a reusable template, you will use the template file setting, identifiable by the .dotx at the end of the file name.

➤ **PDF.** Short for Portable Document Format, this is a file type commonly associated with Adobe products. The .pdf file format is an excellent one to use if you want to send your document to someone who does not have access to Word. You can also send a PDF to someone who is only supposed to read the document without having the ability to edit the text. PDF documents can be opened with free Adobe Acrobat Reader software or other applications.

➤ **Text.** Select the *Plain Text* option to create a text-only version of the document with a .txt suffix. There won't be any page headings, formatting, comments, or other annotations, but the file can be opened and edited on practically any computer using a wide variety of applications.

➤ **Rich Text Format.** This is a hybrid format that allows text documents to have limited formatting, such as bold, bullets, or special fonts applied. Look for .rtf at the end of the file name.

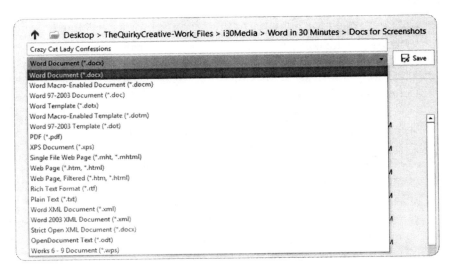

Word Online has just a handful of file formats available via *File > Save As.* The default format is .docx, and there is an option to export a PDF version of the document.

Shutting down

Ready to take a break or shut down for the day? You will want to close out of open Word documents first. Use one of the following methods in Word 2016:

➤ Click the "X" in the upper right corner of the open file (Windows) or the red dot in the upper left corner (macOS).

➤ Select *File > Close.*

➤ Use a keyboard shortcut: Control-W (Windows) or Command-W (Macs)

Be sure to save the document before closing. Word may display a pop-up prompting you to save the newest version:

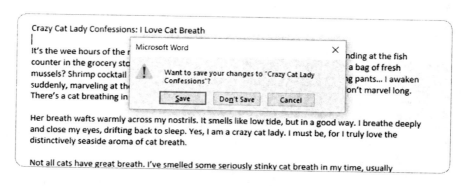

For Word Online, simply shut the browser window or select *Sign Out.* The file will be automatically saved to OneDrive.

Locating a recovered file

If you close out of your file without saving, don't throw yourself in front of a bus. Word 2016 may be able to recover the unsaved version of your file. Sometimes the recovered file will be automatically opened when you relaunch Word. If you don't see it, it may still be found using the following methods.

In Windows, launch Word 2016 and choose *Open Other Documents* from the Start Screen. Then scroll to the bottom of the list of recent documents and select *Recover Unsaved Documents*. Word will search your computer for any available unsaved files. Mac users should select *Recent* in Backstage View and see if the list contains the recovered file.

Printing basics

Unless you are only sharing a document with others as an email attachment or through a cloud service such as OneDrive or Dropbox, you will eventually want to print the document on good, old-fashioned paper. I am always printing to-do and grocery lists, and from time to time I even print out articles I have written for proofing. (I am sure Tegan the Floof would have eventually printed out her pool party flyer if I hadn't interrupted her.)

Before printing a file, it's wise to save it one last time. Then select *File > Print*. Mac users will see the standard Print pop-up, while Windows users will wind up here:

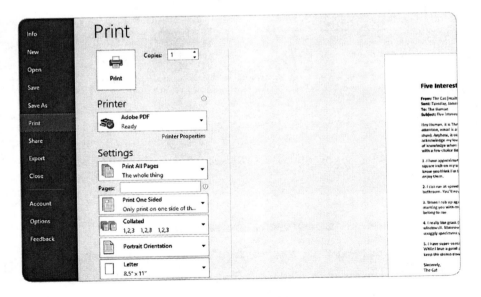

A preview of your document will be displayed on the right two-thirds of the window. You can give the pages a quick once-over using the arrows. On the left side of the window, select a printer (under *Printer*) and how you want to print (under *Settings*). Options include:

➤ **Print All Pages.** Prints the entire document.

➤ **Print Current Page.** Prints the selected page.

➤ **Custom Print.** Enter specific pages or a range of pages to print.

If you only have one printer, you will only need to do this once. You can also change the page orientation and paper size, and adjust the print margins as needed.

Word Online offers a print option via *File > Print*. However, because Word Online uses your computer's browser, you may not be able to print directly to a printer. Instead, you will be prompted to download a PDF of the document, which you can then open in Adobe Acrobat or some other program to print.

Protip: If Word 2016 doesn't print your document, check to see if your printer is turned on. If it still won't print, it may not be correctly configured. I think that's IT code for "pull your hair out and scream." You may be able to open your computer's print settings and troubleshoot the problem, but it may also be necessary to get in touch with someone who knows how to set up printers. A third option: Export the document as a PDF and have the file opened and printed out on someone else's system.

Printing envelopes and labels

In Word 2016, the Mailings tab offers several tools for printing envelopes and address labels:

➤ Select *Envelopes* to enter the destination and return address and set up the printer.

➤ Select *Labels* to enter the information for printing on a sticky address label, such as one that is preprinted with your company name. Several standard sizes are available via the *Options* button.

➤ Once you have entered the relevant data and adjusted the envelope or label settings, select *Print*.

Word Online does not have a Mailings tab or special options for envelopes and labels.

CHAPTER 3

Formatting, layout, and design

Jezebel Kitten, Tegan the Floof, and Gabber T. Tabber are all cats. They all believe they "assist" me at The Quirky Creative, my home-based freelance writing and editing company. And they are all convinced that "assist" means sleeping on whatever I am trying to work on, leaving hairballs in the corners of my office, knocking pens and pencils off my desk, and arguing with each other about whose turn it is to sit on the keyboard.

But other than that, the three cats are actually quite different. Jezebel Kitten is glossy, bold, and black. If she were a font, she would be perfect for attention-grabbing copy. Tegan the Floof is a soft, grey cloud. She insists she is "fluffy" (not fat) and would best be represented by a font with lots of luxurious curves. Gabber T. Tabber, on the other hand, is lithe and quick. When she is not napping, she is almost always chatting to herself. The office comedian, her font style would be welcoming and fun.

If you want to use Word to create documents that are as different as my feline assistants, and more than just uniform strings of sentences on a page, you will need to learn to use the program's formatting and design tools. Fortunately, they are easy to grasp.

How to format individual elements

The individual style elements on the Home tab offer the most straightforward formatting options. There are groups of font and paragraph settings that will enable you to customize the appearance of individual characters as well as paragraphs of text. Settings include:

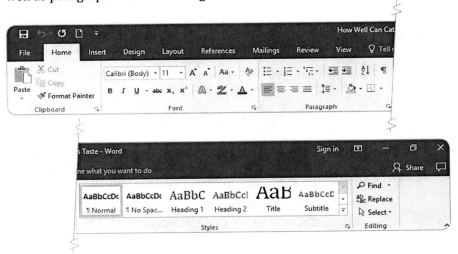

> ➤ **Font and Font Size.** Word offers a number of built-in fonts ranging from the classic to the artistic. When you scroll through your options, you will find fonts arranged by *Theme* (more on this shortly), *Recently Used,* and *All Fonts.* In addition to selecting the font, you can also choose the size (for instance, 11 point Baskerville).

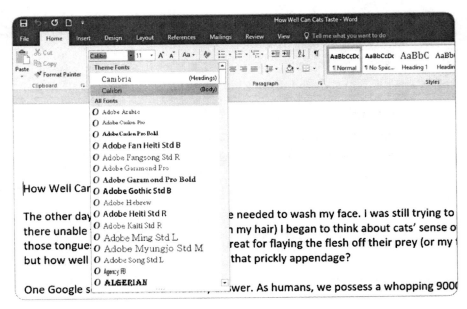

➤ **Bold, Italic and Underline.** These tools do exactly what you expect them to do. In addition to the buttons on the toolbar, it is also possible to use keyboard shortcuts—Control-B for bold, Control-I for italics, and Control-U for underline.

➤ **Text Highlight.** Make portions of your text pop by using this tool to highlight it in a vibrant color.

➤ **Font Color.** Change the color of your text to almost any shade under the sun.

➤ **Bullets, Numbering, and Multileveled Lists.** Use these tools to break up portions of your copy into lists to make your document easier to read. Various styles are offered for each type of list.

➤ **Paragraph Justification.** Choose from *Align Left, Align Right, Center* or *Justify*.

➤ **Line and Paragraph Spacing.** Use this tool to adjust the space between lines as well as add or remove spaces between paragraphs. Reducing line spacing can be particularly useful if you are trying to fit text on a single page but have a bit of overflow.

You can select these settings before you begin typing your document, or after the fact by highlighting text and pressing the relevant toolbar button(s).

Protip: You don't always have to use the formatting tools on the Home tab. For users of the Windows version of Word 2016, the Mini Toolbar is available even if another ribbon is active. To access the Mini Toolbar, simply highlight the text you would like to modify. The Mini Toolbar—which includes font, font size, bold, italic, underline, highlight, and font color settings—will appear. You can also create bulleted and numbered lists and apply styles using the Mini Toolbar.

e?

> The other day, one of my cats decided she needed to wa
> there unable to escape (she was sitting on my hair) I beg
> those tongues covered in tiny barbs are great for flaying
> but how well can they actually taste with that prickly ap

How to format with styles and themes

Let's say you are working on a 20-page report, complete with titles, sub-titles, headings, quotes, and body text. If you wanted to change the fonts and colors for the entire document, you could do it the hard way—by going through every page and selecting paragraphs of text and individual elements and applying the relevant formatting.

However, there is a much easier approach. Word 2016 includes *styles*, pre-set formatting that can be applied to individual text elements, as well as *themes*, which are families of complementary styles. If you apply styles to all of the text elements in your 20-page document (titles, headings, footnotes, body text, etc.), it's possible to instantly change the appearance of the entire document by activating a new theme. It can save lots of time for you, as well as anyone else who might need to work on the document.

Styles

Located on the Home tab, Word's style library lets you quickly apply various styles to selections of text and entire paragraphs.

More styles can be listed by opening the Styles Pane, activated via the *Styles Pane* button (macOS) or the small triangle to the right of the primary styles on the Home tab (Windows and Word Online).

The default style for text in new documents is *Normal*, whose parameters include Calibri font set to 11 points, left-aligned paragraphs without indenting, line spacing of 1.15, and an 8-point blank line between paragraphs. This is the standard body text style.

However, it is possible to apply (or create) another style for body text. I personally prefer *No Spacing* for body text. It uses the same font and font size, and left-aligns paragraphs with no indentation, but spaces lines at 1.0 and does not automatically add a blank line between paragraphs.

Other built-in styles include those for titles, subtitles, quotes, and four levels of headings. You can apply a style using the following methods:

➤ Click on a style listed on the Home tab or Styles Pane before you start typing.

➤ Highlight text and choose a style from the Home tab or Styles Pane.

➤ Highlight text and use one of the style shortcuts listed in the Appendix.

Why is it a good idea to use styles? Besides making it easier to change the formatting of a single line or an entire block of text, styles can also be leveraged by other tools in Word 2016. They include *themes* and *style sets*, described below. Styles are also required for building a table of contents (see Chapter 4).

Modifying styles

From time to time you may want to modify a style. Perhaps the font doesn't work for you, or you want to increase the default indentation. Here's how to do it in Word 2016:

1. Open the Styles Pane.

2. Select the style you want to change.

3. Hover over the name of the style until a drop-down menu appears, and select *Modify*.

4. Make changes to the font, font size, and other settings as needed.

5. Select *Format > Paragraph* to change indentation, spacing, and other special settings.

If you select *Add to Template*, the changes to the style will be carried over to all new documents. In other words, if you increase the font size for the Normal style from 11 to 14 and select *Add to Template*, every time you create a blank document, the Normal style for the new documents will have the same 14-point font. For this reason, it may be better to create a new style, rather than modifying an existing style.

Word Online presents standard styles on the Home tab, but it is not possible to modify them.

How to create a new style

If you are feeling inspired, you can create your own style to use in Word 2016. From the Home tab, open the Styles Pane and select *Create a Style* (Windows) or *New Style* (macOS). You can then set the parameters, from font and font size to alignment, indentation, spacing, and more. After saving the custom style, it will be added to the style library on the Home tab.

Themes

Themes are families of complimentary styles, available to users of Word 2016. By activating a theme, you can apply special formatting to every style in your document. In addition to changing the formatting for document text, themes can also include background colors, design elements, and other effects. This makes it possible to quickly create an attractive, professional-looking document without having to hire a graphic designer. Themes are useful for making a strong impression on your reader, such as when you are creating a résumé or a business report.

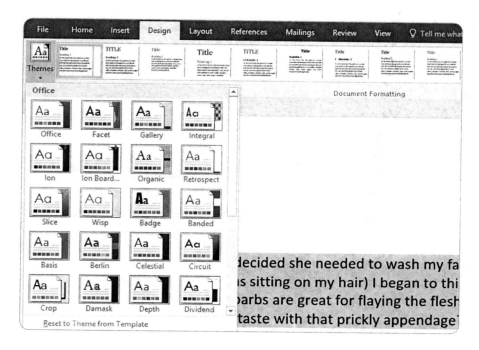

There are more than two dozen built-in themes on the Design tab, each with its own name (Office, Berlin, Ion Boardroom, etc.). Click on the thumbnail at the very left of the Design tab to scroll through the different themes. Once you select a theme, Word will instantly apply the new formatting to the entire document. But remember to apply styles first!

Style sets

An alternative to themes are style sets, which are also found on the Design tab. I won't get into the differences between the two, but just know that like themes, style sets basically allow you to instantly change the appearance of a document. Simply select your favorite from the more than two dozen style sets provided, and the font and paragraph properties of your document will update accordingly.

Neither themes nor style sets are included in Word Online. In addition, Word Online does not have a Design tab.

How to change the page layout

By now you are getting a good picture of the many ways in which you can customize the appearance of text within your Word document using styles, style sets, themes, and individual formatting parameters.

What if you want to spice things up? For instance, let's say you want to create a trifold brochure, which requires three columns on a landscape-oriented page as well as some adjustments to the margins. Don't worry—it's easy to make changes to the layout of your document's pages, using the tools found on the Layout tab in Word 2016:

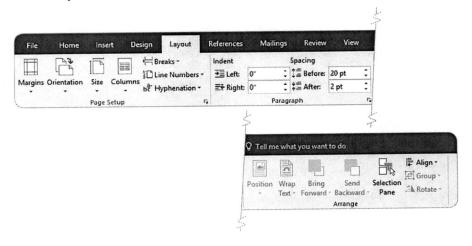

The layout settings I find most useful are:

➤ **Margins.** Select this tool to change the margins on your document's pages. Word includes several common margin settings to choose from. You can also set custom margins.

➤ **Orientation.** Word defaults to portrait orientation for new documents, but there may be times when you actually want to use landscape instead. Change the page orientation when you click on this tool.

➤ **Size.** Select this tool to change the size of your document's pages. Word includes settings for 10 popular paper sizes for you to choose from. You can also set a custom paper size.

➤ **Columns.** If you want to arrange text in your document within multiple columns rather than a single block on a page, you can do so with this tool. Simply click on it and select the number of columns you want to use. You can apply the columns to your entire document or to selected text within it.

Word Online has a Page Layout tab that lets you set margins, orientation, and page size. However, columns and other advanced layout settings are not available.

Working with text

Aside from formatting text, Word has special tools for quickly finding, moving, and replacing individual words and blocks of text. These tools can save loads of time when you are editing a big document.

How to cut, copy, and paste text

If you are working on a document and decide that you need to move a paragraph from the first chapter to the conclusion, you could torture yourself and attempt to do it the hard way—deleting it in one place, and then manually retyping it in its new location.

But there is a much easier way, using tools on the Home tab or keyboard shortcuts. All you need to do is *cut* the text in question in the first chapter, and then move your cursor to the conclusion and *paste* it there. You can also *copy* text that you need to reuse, and paste it into another location or another document. Here is how to cut, copy, and paste text in Word 2016 or Word Online:

Cut. Highlight a word or a group of words, and then select one of these options:

➤ Home tab: Select the scissor icon.

➤ Right-click and select *Cut*.

➤ Use the keyboard shortcuts Control-X (Windows) or Command-X (macOS).

Copy. Highlight a word or a group of words, and then:

➤ Home tab: select the *Copy* button.

➤ Right-click and select *Copy*.

➤ Use the keyboard shortcuts Control-C (Windows) or Command-C (macOS).

Paste. Place the cursor where you want the cut or copied text to appear, and then:

➤ Home tab: use the *Paste* button.

➤ Right-click and select *Paste.*

➤ Use the keyboard shortcuts Control-V (Windows) or Command-V (macOS).

How to find and replace text

Imagine you are writing a screenplay about a cat and a dog whose owners are moving cross-country. When they are dropped off at the airport's pet shipping office, they mistakenly get sent to Auckland, New Zealand, instead of Oakland, California. Hijinks ensue. The cat and the dog (who normally don't like each other) become best friends and solve a major international jewelry robbery before eventually being reunited with their tearful owners in California.

Your Hollywood agent loves the nutty script, except for one thing: The dog, Fritz, can't be a schnauzer. "Trust me on this," he cheerfully says. "Schnauzers don't fight crime. And that kind of dog will look too cute next to the Persian cat, Princess. You need a dog who's bigger and fiercer."

At this point you could manually scroll through the document and remove all 87 references to "schnauzer," and then manually type in the replacement, "German shepherd." But there is a much easier way to handle this, using *Find* and *Replace.*

To find a term in an open document, use one of these methods:

➤ The *Find* button or magnifying glass icon on the Home tab.

➤ The keyboard shortcut Control-F.

To replace a term throughout the document, use the *Replace* button on the Home tab (Windows and Windows Online) or use the keyboard shortcut Control-Shift-H (Windows) or Command-Shift-H (macOS). A small pop-up will appear, with fields to enter the text to be found and replaced (for instance, "schnauzer" and "German shepherd"). You can replace everything all at once, or go through the document to replace (or ignore) each reference as the tool finds the text in question.

The *Replace* button can also be used to correct formatting issues, such as removing extra spaces or replacing short dashes with longer dashes. Use the advanced settings button in the pop-up to look for words with a certain case, specific formatting, or special elements, such as paragraph marks.

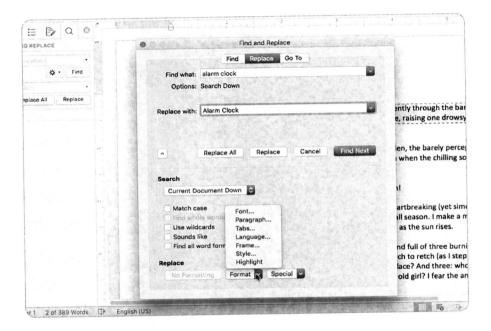

CHAPTER 4

Images, tables, citations, and more

Microsoft understands the importance of visual elements. When you want to connect quickly with your readers and further engage them with the ideas you are trying to convey, additional elements such as pictures, videos, tables, charts, and hyperlinks to web content are more persuasive and attention-getting than mere words.

Add-ons such as cover pages, page breaks, headers and footers, tables of content, and indexes can also increase the navigability of your document. This not only makes it easier for your audience to more quickly understand what the document is about, it can also help them find specific pieces of information.

In decades past, inserting elements into a Word document involved drilling down into various menus. Since Microsoft introduced the Ribbon interface, adding such elements has become much easier. All it takes to get started are a few clicks on the Insert and Reference tabs.

How to add pages

If you are working on a multipage business report, at various locations within your document you may want to add a cover page, blank page, or page break. To add any of these elements in Word 2016, go to the left side of the Insert tab and then take the following steps:

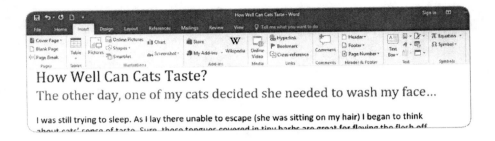

Adding a cover page

➤ Click on the *Cover Page* button.

➤ Select one of the included designs or download additional cover page designs from office.com (Windows only; Internet connection required).

➤ Word will add the selected cover page to the beginning of your document.

➤ Click on each customizable section to edit it.

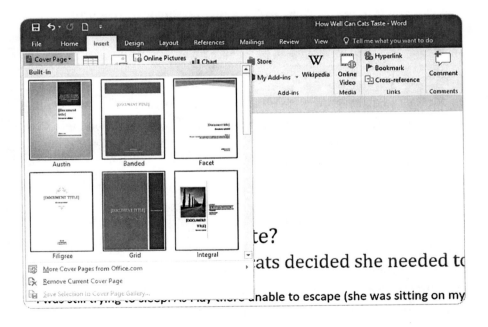

Adding a blank page

➤ Navigate to the location in your Word document where you want the blank page to appear.

➤ Click on *Blank Page.*

➤ Word will add a blank page to your document.

➤ This is a great option if you want to leave room for written notes on the printed document, or make space for a full-page photo, table, or chart.

Adding a page break

➤ Navigate to the location in your Word document where you want the page to end.

➤ Select *Page Break* on the Insert tab.

➤ Word will end the page at that location and move your cursor (and any text that follows it) to a new page.

➤ Page breaks are useful in documents with multiple sections that require each section to begin on its own page, such as the chapters of this book.

Word Online only includes a *Page Break* button on the Insert tab.

Getting tabular with tables

Tables are great for presenting a neatly organized set of information in a document. For instance, if you wanted to present a chart showing the average number of hours your cats sleep every day, you could create something like this in your Word document:

Cat	Hours/day sleeping
Jezebel Kitten	11.5
Tegan the Floof	17
Gabber T. Tabber	14

The *Table* button, located on the left side of the Insert tab, makes it easy to add a table. In fact, there are multiple ways to add a table using this button. First, place your cursor where you want the table to appear, and click the *Table* button. Then:

➤ Use your cursor to select the number of rows and columns you want your table to contain. Click again, and Word will insert the table into your document. This method can be used in Word 2016 as well as Word Online.

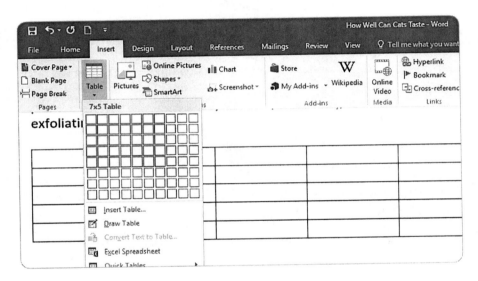

➤ Select *Insert Table* (Word 2016 only) and enter your chosen number of rows and columns in the pop-up that appears. Click *OK* and Word will add the table to your document.

➤ Select *Draw Table* (Word 2016 only). Your cursor will turn into a pencil. Use the cursor to draw a large rectangle for your table's border. Then use it to draw horizontal lines for rows and vertical lines for columns.

➤ Select *Excel Spreadsheet* (Word 2016 for Windows only). When you click outside the spreadsheet pop-up, Word will convert it into a table embedded in your document.

➤ Select *Quick Tables* and choose from a number of built-in options (Word 2016 for Windows only).

If you have entered text in your document and later decide it would work well as a table, you can easily convert it to one (Word 2016 only):

1. Highlight the text with your cursor.
2. Click the *Table* button.
3. Choose *Convert Text to Table*.
4. Enter the number of rows and columns needed in the pop-up.

To add text to any table, just click inside any cell and begin to type. You can format the text with stylistic elements exactly as you have learned to do with the rest of the copy in your document.

Modifying a table

Once you have created a table, Word has made it easy for you to make modifications such as adding columns and rows or changing the design and layout. You can make these changes using the contextual tabs that appear when you are working on a table in both Word 2016 and Word Online.

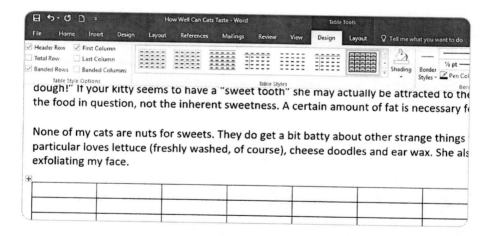

The Design tab has tools to modify the table's style. Options in Word 2016 include shading, gridlines, borders, and formatting for rows and columns. The Layout tab includes tools to insert additional rows and columns, adjust the height and width of cells, align table text, and even sort or apply mathematical formulas. There is also a tool to merge cells, which comes in handy for creating headers that stretch across more than one column.

You can also make limited changes to a table using the Mini Toolbar. To access the Mini Toolbar while working with a table, simply right click with your mouse. You can use the Mini Toolbar to add or remove shading, borders, and rows and columns quickly and efficiently.

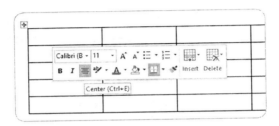

Word Online also has contextual tabs for Design and Layout, but the feature set is more limited.

Charting new territory with charts

Sometimes you may want to add an element that not only conveys more information than a simple table, but also makes a bigger visual impact. Word 2016 has just the ticket for you: charts. The software can add all kinds of charts, from simple column, line, and pie charts to more complex histogram, waterfall, funnel and combo charts.

For the sake of explanation, I will walk you through the creation of a simple chart—in this case, a pie chart illustrating how my cats spend an average day. Note that the chart tool is only available in Word 2016, not Word Online.

Start by clicking the *Chart* button on the Insert tab, and then choose *Pie*. This reveals several pie chart options, from a three-dimensional pie chart to a doughnut. We will stick with the basic Pie option for now:

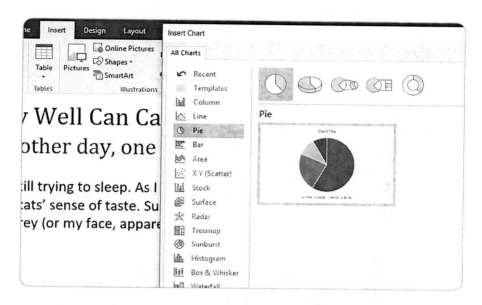

At this point, Word 2016 will turn to another Microsoft Office application, Excel, to build the chart. An Excel spreadsheet will appear containing some default data. As we replace the default data with the details of my cats' daily agenda, we are rewarded with a colorful pie chart. After the data is entered, close the spreadsheet and the chart will be complete:

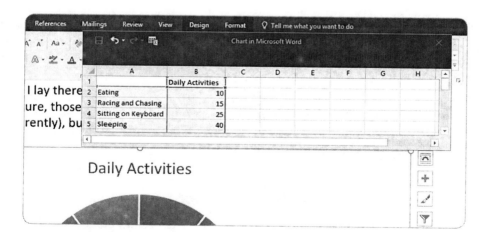

As with photos and other image files, you can move the chart by clicking on it and dragging it to a new location in your document. Resize it by dragging one of the circles at the top, bottom, sides, or corners. You have the same options for wrapping text as well.

Making changes to your chart

If you are happy with the data in your chart but want to adjust its appearance, Word 2016 has you covered. When you click on the chart, *Chart Elements*, *Chart Styles* and *Chart Filters* will appear next to your work of art:

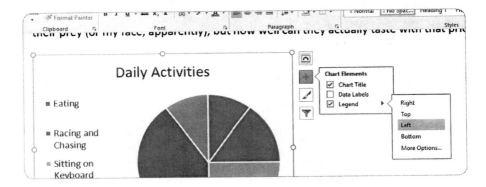

➤ Select or deselect *Chart Elements* to quickly change the *Chart Title*, *Data Labels* and *Legend*. Clicking on the arrow to the right of each element reveals additional placement options.

➤ Select *Chart Styles* to customize your chart's colors or choose from a multitude of predesigned styles.

➤ Use *Chart Filters* to edit the data points and names. Uncheck the boxes of any data points or names you wish to hide. Click *Select Data* in the lower right corner of the pop-up to bring back the spreadsheet that contains the data.

Contextual tabs for charts

Inserting a chart into your document reveals two contextual tabs. The Design tab includes tools for quickly adding chart elements, changing the layout and style, and editing chart data:

The Format tab includes tools for inserting shapes and word art as well as arranging, wrapping, and aligning your chart with the document's text:

How to add cat pictures (and other images) to your document

Tables and charts are good for displaying and explaining data. However, sometimes a picture can be worth a thousand words, especially if it includes a cat or some other furry companion. Word has made it easy to add images to any document using the Pictures tool, located on the Insert tab. To add an image file to your document, follow these steps:

1. In your open document, click on the location where the image is supposed to appear.

2. Select the *Pictures* button on the Insert tab.

3. Navigate to wherever your image is stored on your PC, OneDrive, or other storage location.

4. Select the image file and click *Insert*.

5. Word will embed the image in your document.

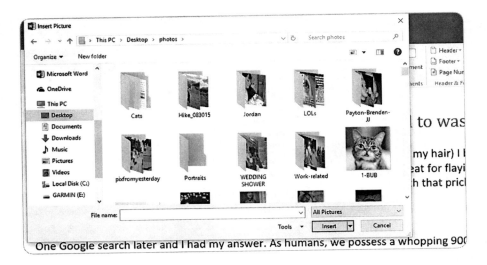

Once an image is embedded in your document, select it and Word will activate a contextual tab, Picture Format. This ribbon has all kinds of tools for editing the image and changing its appearance on the page. It includes settings for resizing and cropping the image. You can add borders and artistic effects, such as shadows and three-dimensional elements. You can also adjust how the picture will affect the text around it using the *Wrap Text* button (Word 2016 only). These options are explained in more detail below.

Wrapping text

When you place an image on a page, it's not necessary to have it sitting on its own line, sandwiched between text. If you want to produce a document with a more professional design using Word 2016, you can wrap the text around images. Here's how:

1. Select an image and switch to the Picture Format tab.
2. Click the *Wrap Text* button or *Position* button.
3. Select the text wrapping option that looks best.

Resizing the picture

To change the size of the picture in your document, select the image and drag the corners until it is the size that you like. Or, switch to the Picture Format tab and use the resizing tools on the right side of the Ribbon.

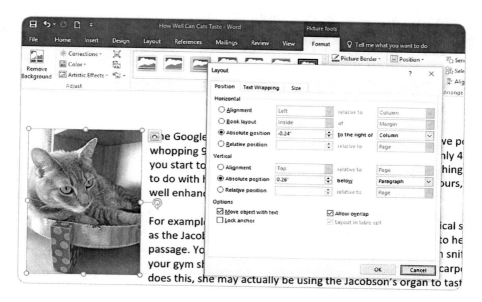

Moving the picture

To move the picture to a new location in your document, simply select the image and drag it to the location where you would like it to appear.

Protip: The Windows version of Word 2016 and Word Online allow users to insert images from online sources. You can retrieve images from OneDrive, Flickr, Facebook, or Bing image search. To get started, choose the *Online Pictures* button on the Insert tab and follow the directions that appear.

Mixing in some cat videos
(or other online media)

From a tiny kitten that cuddles up with the family dog, to otherwise stalwart felines who flee at the sight of cucumbers, I just can't get enough cat videos. So much so, in fact, that I sometimes feel compelled to add a short cat video to a Word document.

If you ever get a similar urge, inserting online media is as simple as navigating to the Insert tab and selecting *Online Video* (Word 2016 for Windows only). Word will present options to use Bing or YouTube to search for the video you want, or paste in a video embed code from YouTube or some other source.

Once you have found the video you want to use, select it and click *Insert*. Word will establish a link between your Word document and the online video. This link will appear as an image. You can move it, resize it and adjust the layout options using the same methods you used for tables, charts, and pictures. When a reader clicks the *Play* button within the image, his or her computer will open a video viewer and play the video as long as the computer or device is connected to the Internet.

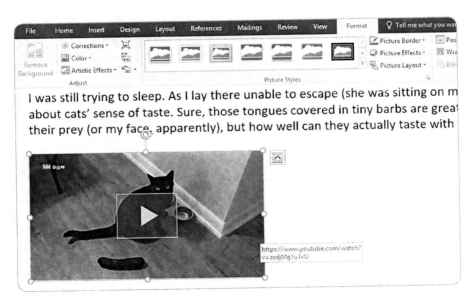

If you have the Mac version of Word 2016, you will not see the online video option on the Insert tab. Instead, there will be a *Media* button to insert video and audio files from a local hard drive or network storage location. Word Online does not have any options for inserting video into a document.

How to add a hyperlink

As much as I love cat photos, cat videos, and pie charts about cats, the most common element I add to my Word documents are *hyperlinks*. A hyperlink is a neat little bit of code that, when clicked upon, enables your reader to instantly jump to a page on the Internet, another location in the current document, or another document. You can also use hyperlinks to open a blank Word document, or compose an email. In my line of work, I generally use hyperlinks to link to online sources of statistics and other data I quote in my articles and reports.

As with just about everything else in Word, adding a hyperlink is easy. In fact, whenever you type in a website or email address, Word will automatically add the hyperlink for you. How can you tell? The hyperlinked text will turn blue and be underlined.

You can also manually attach a hyperlink to any word or sentence in your document. To do so, follow these steps:

1. Highlight the text with your cursor.

2. Right-click and select *Hyperlink* or navigate to the Insert tab and click *Hyperlink* (Word 2016) or *Link* (Word Online).

A pop-up window will appear with options to add a link to a file (such as a PDF, spreadsheet, or another Word document), a web page (browse to the address or type the URL in the field provided), a location in the document, or an email address. The *Text to display* field will contain the text you high-lighted. Click *OK* (Word 2016) or *Insert* (Word Online) to create the link.

Here's what the pop-up looks like for users of Word 2016 for Windows:

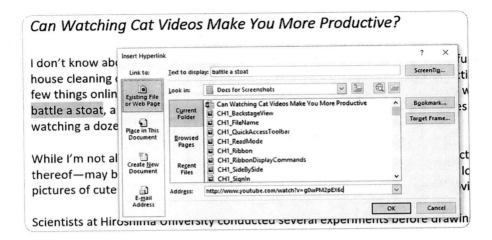

Word 2016 also gives users the option of adding a hyperlink to another location in the same document:

1. Select *Place in This Document* (Windows) or *This Document* (macOS) from the pop-up menu.

2. Choose the heading in the document that you want the reader to jump to. In order to do so, you will need to have previously applied headings and other styles to the document.

I have occasionally used this type of hyperlink to give my reader the option to jump to a reference chart or table located elsewhere in the document.

Once you have added a hyperlink, right-click on it to *Edit, Open, Copy,* or *Remove* the link.

> **Protip:** If you choose to hyperlink one document to another, your reader will need access to both documents in order for the hyperlink to work.

How to add headers and footers

Multipage documents such as term papers, quarterly reports, and book manuscripts can benefit from the addition of headers and footers. These elements can make a really big difference in the appearance of your document, turning a plain-looking report into something that looks professional and polished. Navigate to the Insert tab to get started.

To add a header to your document in Word 2016, click on the *Header* button. From there you can select one of the many built-in header designs. Windows users can also choose to download additional headers from office.com.

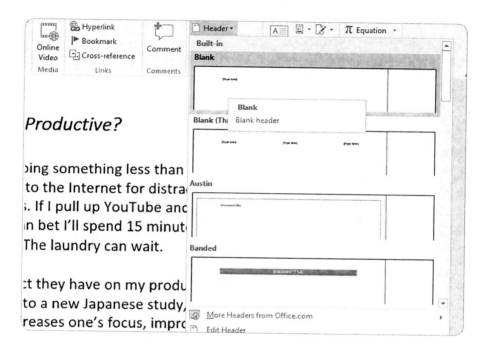

Once you have found a design you like, a single click is all it takes to add it to the document for editing. You can then use the contextual tab for headers and footers to adjust the header's position or add the following elements to the header:

➤ Page numbers.

➤ Date and time stamp.

➤ Document info.

➤ Images.

➤ Different headers for odd or even pages.

To replace the default text within the header, just click on each placeholder and type in your own. Click the *Close* button when you are done.

To add a footer to your document, select *Footer* on the Insert tab and then follow the same steps using the contextual tab for headers and footers.

Users of Word Online can also insert headers and footers, but there are no fancy designs or placement options to choose from. Press the *Header & Footer* button on the Insert tab, and enter text in the fields provided. The *Options* button gives a few additional options, including the ability to use alternating headers on odd and even pages.

How to add page numbers

To add page numbers to your document, follow these steps:

1. Select *Page Number* on the Insert tab.

2. Choose where you would like the page number to appear (*Top of Page*, *Bottom of Page*, *Page Margins*, or *Current Position*).

3. Select the page number design that appeals to you.

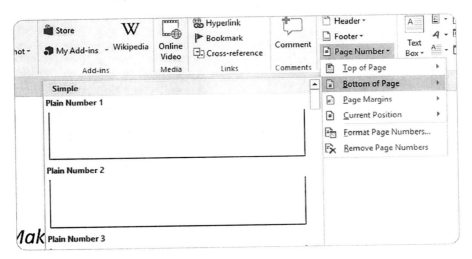

Word Online users can also insert page numbers using the same button on the Insert tab, but there are limited placement and design options.

What if you decide you don't like having a header, footer, or page numbers in your document? Just click the appropriate option on the Insert tab and select *Remove Header, Remove Footer,* or *Remove Page Number* from the menu (Word 2016) or *Options* in Word Online.

How to add a table of contents

Longer documents with multiple chapters, sections, and subsections—such as a book manuscript, business report, or dissertation—can also benefit from a table of contents (TOC). A good TOC can make it a lot easier for your readers to find what they are looking for. Word 2016 can automatically build a TOC, though headings and other styles must first be applied to the various sections of your document. We talked about how to do this in Chapter 3, so feel free to go back for a quick refresher.

To add a new table of contents to your document, follow these steps:

1. Place your cursor on the first page of your document.

2. Open the References tab.

3. Click the *Table of Contents* button on the left side of the Ribbon.

4. Select from one of the built-in styles.

In the blink of an eye, your table of contents will appear, complete with page numbers and embedded hyperlinks for each section listed.

Contents

If you later make changes to headings or add or remove content, you can update the table of contents in a flash. Just click on the TOC and select *Update Table* on the References tab. You can then choose whether you only want to only update page numbers or the entire table to reflect changes in headings and subheadings. I continually edit what I have written, so I always use the second option to make sure my TOC remains as accurate as possible.

Word Online does not have a References tab or a tool to automatically build a table of contents.

How to add a footnote or endnote

On some occasions you may want to add footnotes or endnotes to your document in order to cite reference sources or provide additional comments for readers. Such citations are required for many types of academic papers, essays, business reports, and nonfiction books.

The only significant difference between a footnote or an endnote is the placement. A footnote will appear at the bottom of the page, while an endnote will appear at the end of your document. I personally tend to use footnotes when I want to add an interesting comment because they are more likely to get the reader's immediate attention. I lean toward endnotes for citations, as they are less likely to interrupt the flow of what I have written.

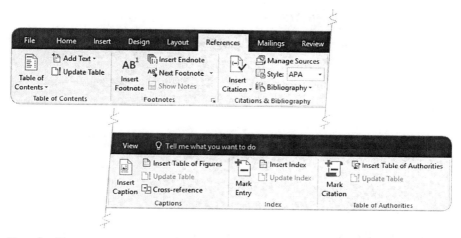

Use the Footnotes section of the References tab to add footnotes and end-notes to your document:

1. Place your cursor at the end of the sentence that contains the information you wish to comment upon or provide a citation for.

2. Select *Insert Footnote* or *Insert Endnote*.

3. Microsoft Word will place a number in superscript (like this[1]) next to the final word as well as the corresponding number at the bottom of the page or end of the document.

4. Type in the information you want the footnote or endnote to contain.

If you click on the arrow in the lower right-hand corner of the Footnotes section of the References tab, you can access additional formatting options. These include location, layout, and number format.

Word Online can also add footnotes and endnotes, but the buttons are on the Insert tab (there is no References tab in Word Online). Select *Show Footnotes > Format Options* to change fonts and other formatting.

Word will automatically update the footnote and endnote numbers in your document to ensure they are sequential. If you decide you want to delete a footnote or endnote, simply highlight the superscript number in the text and hit the Backspace or Delete key on your keyboard.

Citations and bibliographies

Students, researchers, and other academic types often use in-text citations and bibliographies in their documents. Word 2016 has a great toolset to organize citations and automatically build a bibliography. It's located on the References tab.

The first thing to understand about these tools is that you have to create citations in order to add a bibliography to the document. It's easy to do:

1. Place the cursor where you want the citation to appear.

2. Go to the References tab and select *Insert Citation*.

3. Select the type of source (book, journal article, website, etc.) using the drop-down menu.

4. Enter the information into the form. Some fields, such as author and title, are required.

5. Click *OK*.

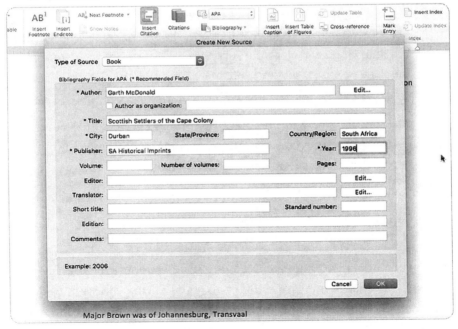

A citation will appear in the text. The default style is *(author, year)* but you can edit what is shown by double-clicking on it. You can also delete the in-text citation using your keyboard, but the citation will still be available to insert elsewhere—click the *Citations* button on the References tab, and double-click one of the listed citations to place it where the text is located.

To add a bibliography to the end of the document, all you need to do is select *Bibliography* from the References tab. Pick one of the designs shown, and the bibliography will automatically populate with data drawn from your references list. Even better, you can use the adjoining drop-down menu to select the listing style—for instance, MLA or Chicago.

About the only thing missing from the citation/bibliography tool is integration with citation-style footnotes. But there is a manual workaround—simply copy and paste the bibliography listing into reference-style footnotes. Some follow-up formatting may be required, however.

Word Online does not have any citation or bibliography tools.

How to add an index

If you have ever paged through a reference book—such as a textbook or a recipe book—you have probably encountered an index. Located at the end of a document or in the back of a book, it is a list of words or phrases along with corresponding page numbers.

Readers can turn to the index to find specific topics within the document. If you ever have the need, you can use the Index tools on Word 2016's References tab to add an index list to your document. In fact, the index at the end of this book was created using Word 2016.

Marking index entries

To create an index, you must first read through your copy and mark each word and/or phrase to be included in the index. Marking an entry involves the following steps:

1. Highlight the selected text with your cursor.

2. Select *Mark Entry* in the References tab. This will reveal the *Mark Index Entry* pop-up, which includes options for changing the text, adding subentries and cross-references, and more.

3. Click *Mark* to mark the selected text for the index or *Mark All* to mark the selected text as well as all instances of matching text throughout your document.

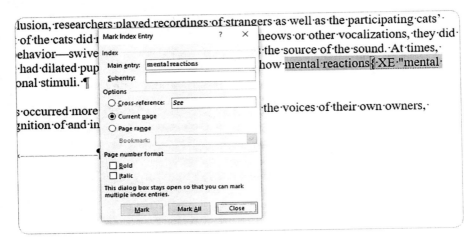

Word 2016 will insert a bit of code around each marked word or phrase. Don't worry—the code will not appear in the printed document. To hide the code from view while it is on-screen, click the *Hide/Show* tool (the paragraph symbol, "¶") to deactivate it.

The *Mark Index Entry* pop-up will remain open as you scroll through your document and continue marking words and phrases for inclusion in the index. When you have marked everything you want to include, you can close the pop-up.

Alternately, you can close the pop-up after each entry and then add new words to the index each time you encounter one. Note that there is a keyboard shortcut to speed up the process of creating an index (see Appendix).

Inserting the index

Once you have marked your index entries, it is time to add the actual index to your document. Place your cursor at the end of the document (if that is where you want the index to reside) and click on *Insert Index* on the References tab. An *Index* pop-up window will appear that lets you scroll through available formats as well as change the columns and language. Once you have selected the format you want, click *OK* to add the index.

As with the table of contents, you can update the index with a simple click of a button whenever you make changes to your document or manually mark new entries. Just select *Update Index* on the References tab once you are done.

These features are only available in the Windows and macOS versions of Word 2016. Word Online does not have a tool for creating an index.

CHAPTER 5

Review and collaboration

By now you have learned how versatile Word 2016 can be. This powerful word processing application makes it easy to apply everything from basic formatting to detailed charts and source citations. You have learned how to leverage images, headers, and charts to create eye-catching documents for work, school, and home.

But we are not quite done. If you are as much of a perfectionist and stickler for details as I am, you are going to absolutely love the features Microsoft has included in Word 2016 (and Word Online) to enable anyone to greatly reduce the number of typos, spelling errors, and grammar problems. There are also tools that enable collaboration with colleagues, classmates, and friends. You will find most of them on the Review tab.

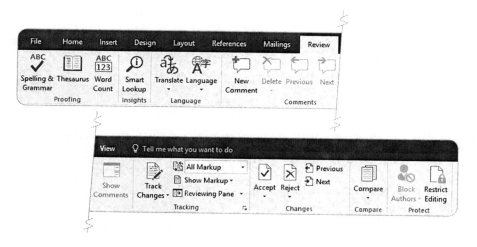

How to check spelling and grammar

Consider the following sentences:

There cat had six toes on each of it's paws. The lepard stocked through a field of blooming flours.

In the old days, reading these two sentences would make you want to throw your dictionary and dog-eared copy of *The Elements of Style* against the wall … and then promptly pick them up to correct and improve the sentences. Nowadays, Word has features to correct spelling and grammar mistakes. Even if you pride yourself on producing spotless drafts, using the tools on the Review tab can give you the peace of mind that repetitive proofreading with your own eyeballs may not (especially after midnight).

There are two ways to check the spelling and grammar in your Word document:

Automatic. By default, Word automatically checks spelling and grammar as you type. It will underline potential misspellings in red and possible grammatical mistakes in blue. When you right-click on the underlined word, you can choose to ignore the suggested correction, or in the case of spelling, add the word to Word's dictionary.

Spelling & Grammar. You can run a spelling and grammar check on your entire document at any time by clicking the *Spelling & Grammar* button on the left side of the Review tab in Word 2016. Doing so will open the *Proofing Pane*. For each potential error, you will be given the option to *Ignore* or *Change*. You can also *Add* the word to your custom dictionary (useful for unrecognized words and proper nouns). When grammar errors are encountered, Word 2016 will provide an explanation for suggested corrections.

Word Online has a *Spelling* button located on the Review tab. The tool can make suggestions for misspelled words, but there is also the ability to add new terms to a custom dictionary by clicking the *Add* button. In addition, Word Online cannot currently check your document's grammar.

ason is Here Again

eaceful. An early spring breeze wafts gently through the barely open window,
comforter all the more delicious. I wake, raising one drowsy eyelid a scant
tently. What was that sound?

the steady ticking of the clock in the den, the barely perceptible drip-drip-drip
l is well. I prepare to drift off again when the chilling sound echoes down the
urgha! Hurgha!" That's right, it's hairball season.

gles the start of baseball season, the heartbreaking (yet simultaneously hilarious)
ingles the beginning of hairball season. I make a mental note to administer a
e family members as soon as the sun rises.

larm clock, I exit my bedroom with mind full of three burning questions. One:
with the heaviest foot traffic upon which to retch (as I step in cold, congealed ca
plagued with hairballs in the first place? And three: who the heck is Justin

Protip: In Word 2016, spelling and grammar tools can be customized or disabled in *Options > Proofing* in Backstage View (Windows) or *Word > Preferences > Spelling* (macOS). From there you can customize Word's AutoCorrect feature as well as adjust settings related to spelling and grammar. Select *Custom Dictionaries > Edit Word List* to remove words that were accidentally added to your custom dictionary.

Using comments for editing and collaboration

As my grandmother used to say, "Opinions are like noses—we all have one." Word comments are a great way to attach opinions, questions, thoughts, and additional details to specific parts of your document. Comments can serve as reminders to yourself when you get around to refining a document, or they can facilitate collaboration and editing with others.

Add a comment by highlighting a piece of text and then clicking on the *New Comment* button on the Review tab. Type your comment into the balloon that appears in the right margin of your document.

Other comment tools include:

➤ **Show Comments.** Display all comments alongside the document.

➤ **Previous.** Jump to the previous comment in the document.

➤ **Next.** Jump to the next comment in the document.

➤ **Delete.** This tool includes a drop-down menu from which you can choose to *Delete All Comments* Shown or *Delete All Comments in Document.*

When collaborating with others, you can respond to a colleague's comment by clicking inside it and selecting *Reply.* From there, just type your response in the space provided.

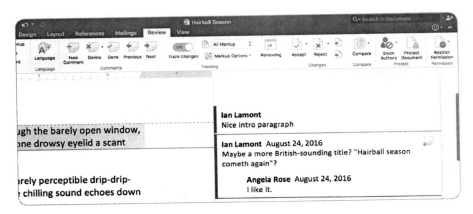

Protip: The only way to remove comments from your document is to delete them. While you can temporarily hide them with some of the tracking discussed in the next section, hidden comments will reappear the next time you—or someone else—opens the document.

The dreaded red pen: working with tracking

If you ever submitted a term paper in school and had it returned covered with comments and corrections in red ink, you know the despair the dreaded red pen can cause. Fortunately, Word 2016 has a way to make editing and revising less painful. It's called tracking. You will find tracking tools on the Review tab.

How to turn tracking on and off

Whether you have been asked to collaborate on a colleague's document or you plan to share your own, you can use the tracking tools to keep track of all changes made to the content, including:

- ➤ New text

- ➤ Deleted words

- ➤ Formatting changes

- ➤ Changes to tabs, headers, footnotes, and other inserted elements

To activate tracking, use the *Track Changes* button on the Review tab. To turn it off, click it a second time.

Tracking is not available to users of Word Online. While there is a *Show Edit Activity* button on Word Online's Review tab, it does not work well—I was unable to view my own edit history or that of collaborators on a test document.

Restricting collaboration and setting passwords

For the Windows version of Word 2016, click the little arrow on the *Track Changes* button to *Lock Tracking*. Doing so prevents your collaborators from turning off tracking unless they enter a password you create.

The Review tab has several additional tools you can use to limit the actions of collaborators. In the Windows version of Word 2016, click the *Restrict Editing* button to limit formatting to a selection of styles, prevent editing, or require tracking. Highlight text you don't want anyone to edit with your cursor and then click the *Block Authors* button to prevent collaborators from making any changes to that section of the document.

Users of the Mac version of Word 2016 have the *Block Authors* button, too. To restrict collaborators' editing options, select *Protect Document* and use the checkboxes under *Protection*. It is also possible to create a password using the *Protect Document* button. Unless collaborators have the password, they will be unable to open the document.

Word Online does not have these features, but by default, a document stored in OneDrive and accessed via Word Online can only be opened by you.

Choosing what to review

Once tracking has been activated in Word 2016, you will have several options for viewing the changes that were made. On the Review tab, use the *Display for Review* tool (Windows) or *Markup* menu (macOS) to choose which changes to display.

➤ **Simple Markup.** Only comments are displayed in the right margin, and a color-coded bar will appear to the left of each paragraph in which changes have been made.

➤ **All Markup.** New text will be colored and underlined. Deleted text will appear with a strikethrough, or in the right margin. These revision marks are color-coded for each user, making it easy to see who made each change. Word will also note any changes made to the formatting. Comments appear in the right margin.

➤ **No Markup.** View the changed document without the revision marks.

➤ **Original.** View the original document without any of the changes or the revision marks.

Use the *Show Markup* tool (Windows) or the *Markup Options* drop-down (macOS) to select specific types of changes to display, such as *Comments, Insertions and Deletions*, and *Formatting*. This tool can also isolate changes made by specific reviewers.

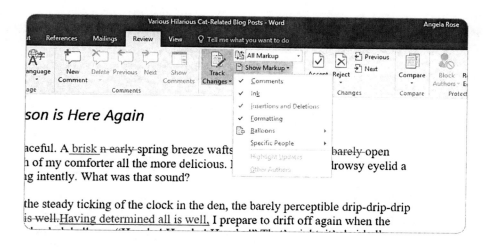

You can also activate the *Reviewing Pane* tool (Windows) or *Reviewing* button (macOS) from the Review tab. It offers a quick way to scan through comments and changes without having to scroll through the entire document to find them.

Accepting and rejecting changes

Once your document has gone through the editing process, it will be time to deal with your collaborators' changes. Once again, you will find the tools you need on the Review tab:

> **Accept.** Accept changes one at a time or all at once. There is also an option to *Accept and Move to Next*, which is a faster way to review each change in the document.

> **Reject.** Reject changes one at a time or all at once.

> **Previous.** Go back to the previous tracked change.

> **Next.** Jump forward to the next tracked change.

You can also right-click over any change made in the document and choose *Accept Insertion* or *Reject Insertion* (or *Accept Deletion* or *Reject Deletion*).

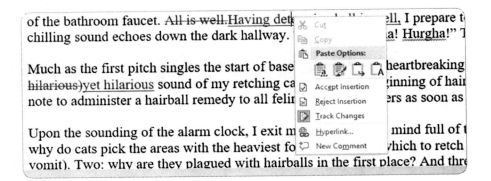

Protip: Tracked changes can be printed in color, or saved as a PDF. Many users like to print *redline* versions of their documents along with clean versions (using the *No Markup* option described earlier) to present to clients, bosses, lawyers, or other parties who want a record of the revisions.

Protecting your work

Word 2016 includes several features to protect your documents. In Windows, they are accessed via the Info tab of the Backstage View menu. Mac users can use the *Protect Document* button on the Review tab. Selecting *Protect Document* will enable you to:

➤ **Mark as Final** (Windows) or **Read Only** (macOS). Selecting this option will convert your document to read-only and prevent anyone else from making changes without creating a new copy first.

➤ **Encrypt with Password** (Windows) or **Password** (macOS). This will set a password that all users must enter in order to open the document. Don't forget the password, or you may not be able to access your own document!

As mentioned earlier, Word Online does not have the same document protection features, but by default a document stored in OneDrive and accessed via Word Online can only be opened by you.

Users of Word 2016 for Windows have several additional options in *Backstage View > Info > Protect Document*:

➤ **Restrict Editing.** This is another way to access the *Restrict Editing* tool on the Review tab.

➤ **Add a Digital Signature.** If you have a digital ID, use this tool to add it to your document. Digital IDs are used to validate your identity, proving that you are the author of the document in question. You can purchase a digital ID from several Microsoft partners including Docu-Sign and GlobalSign.

➤ **Inspect Document.** *Check for Issues and Inspect Document* (available from *Backstage View > Info*) will prompt Word to search your document for personal information you may not want to share with others as well as comments and changes you may have forgotten to delete, accept, or reject.

Collaboration using shared documents

If you have ever tried to write a business letter, report, or article that required input from other people, you know about the wasted time and confusion associated with emailing documents back and forth. It can be very frustrating to produce a final draft that takes into account all of the comments and edits made by multiple contributors. Disaster can strike if you accidentally send the wrong version of a document to someone in the chain.

Microsoft's programmers feel your pain. They have made huge strides with new features that make it relatively easy to share documents and collaborate.

To use Word's collaboration features, you must first share your document. To do so from Word 2016 or Word Online, click the Share icon (which looks like a silhouette) in the upper right corner of the Ribbon (Windows users can also share from Backstage View). You can invite people to access a shared copy of the document using a cloud storage service, such as Microsoft's OneDrive, or you can send an email attachment. If the document is not already stored in the cloud, you will be prompted to save it to OneDrive.

If you want to collaborate in real-time, with more than one person working on the document at the same time, you will need to save the document to OneDrive or another online service such as Dropbox or iCloud. If you choose to send an attachment, you will be given the option to send a Word document or a PDF copy of the document.

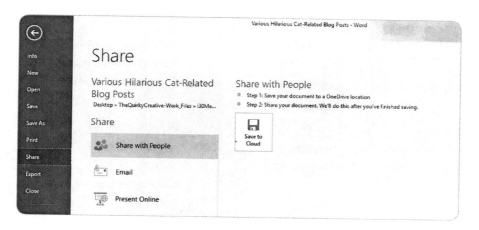

Collaboration options

If you upload the document to a cloud storage service such as OneDrive, Word will prompt you to enter the email addresses of the people you would like to share the file with. For each address, you can designate *Can Edit* (if you would like them to be able to make changes to the document) or *Can View* (a read-only copy). You can also enter a message to your collaborator(s) that Word will send along with a link to the shared file.

An Internet connection is required to access the shared document, but collaborators do not need to have a Microsoft account. Once a collaborator clicks on the link and starts editing, you can work on the document at the same time or separately. The shared file can be accessed on any device with Word installed, including PCs, laptops, tablets, and smartphones. If your collaborators don't have Word, they can use Word Online for free. However, collaboration features may not work correctly for people who are using older versions of Word.

Live collaboration

If you and at least one other collaborator want to see each other's changes as they are made, each of you will have to choose *Yes* when Word asks you if you want to automatically share changes as they happen. Color-coded flags will let you know where each person is working within the document. Word will also alert you when collaborators open or close the file.

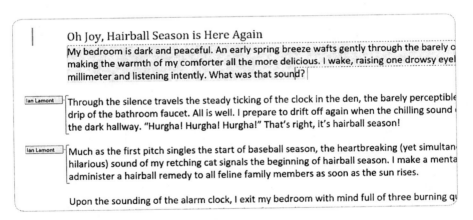

Of all of the updates to Word since the last version of the software, live collaboration is one of the most useful and time-saving features.

Conclusion

In the past 30 minutes, you have learned how to navigate Word 2016's user interface, create new files from a blank page or template, use many of the nifty tools located on the Ribbon, and make the most of Word's stellar review and collaboration features. You also know how to build a table of contents and an index, add footnotes and endnotes, and even protect your document from unwanted edits.

Now it is time to put this new knowledge to work, whether your ultimate goal is to impress a potential employer with an eye-catching résumé, astonish your boss with a gorgeous report, wow a teacher with a well-organized research paper, or just create beautifully designed documents for your own use. Whenever you need to put metaphorical pen to paper, Word 2016—and *Microsoft Word In 30 Minutes*—will be there for you.

I have enjoyed sharing my experience with you, and I hope you have had as much fun reading this guide as I had writing it. You can learn more about me at my website, www.thequirkycreative.com, or by looking me up on LinkedIn (www.linkedin.com/in/thequirkycreative). I would love to see what you are doing with Word—especially if you throw in a cat photo, video or anecdote—so please don't hesitate to drop me a line.

Thanks for reading!

P.S. If you are happy with the knowledge you have gained from *Microsoft Word In 30 Minutes*, please let other people know about it, either by leaving an honest review online or recommending this guide to your personal and professional networks.

About the author

Angela Rose is a writer and B2C marketing strategist based in Colorado. When she's not removing cats from her keyboard, you can find Angela searching for the perfect taco, running 5Ks, whipping up original pastry recipes, and hiking the Colorado Mountains with her photographer husband.

Angela is also the author of *LinkedIn In 30 Minutes (2nd Edition)*.

Keyboard Shortcuts

Word 2016 Universal Shortcuts (Windows/macOS)

CONTROL + B — Bold text

CONTROL + I — Italicize text

CONTROL + U — Underline text

CONTROL + A — Select all

CONTROL + F — Find text

CONTROL + H — Find and replace

CONTROL + Z — Undo

CONTROL + Y — Redo

CONTROL + X — Cut selected cells, text, numbers, and formatting

CONTROL + C — Copy selected cells, text, numbers, and formatting

CONTROL + V — Paste

CONTROL + P — Print

TAB — Indent

ESC — Cancel

Additional Windows Shortcuts

CONTROL + N — New document

CONTROL + O — Open file

CONTROL + S — Save file

CONTROL + W — Close document

CONTROL + E — Center text

CONTROL + L — Left-align text

Control + R — Right-align text

Control + K — Insert link

Control + Shift + E — Activate/deactivate tracking

Control + Left Arrow — Move cursor one word to the left

Control + Right Arrow — Move cursor one word to the right

Control + Up Arrow — Move cursor to the start of the previous paragraph

Control + Down Arrow — Move cursor to the start of the next paragraph

Control + Home — Beginning of document

Control + End — End of document

Control + Backspace — Delete one word to the left

Control + Delete — Delete one word to the right

Control + Enter — Insert page break

Page Up — Up one screen

Page Down — Down one screen

Shift + F3 — Toggle case of selected text

Alt — Select active ribbon. Arrow keys move to adjoining ribbons.

Tab or *Shift + Tab* — Move focus to commands on Ribbon.

Alt + F — Backstage View

Alt + H — Home tab

Alt + N — Insert tab

Alt + G — Design tab

Alt + P — Layout tab

Alt + S — References tab

Alt + M — Mailings tab

Alt + R — Review tab

Alt + W — View tab

Alt + Q — Go to "Tell me . . ." box

Alt + R, C — Insert comment

Alt + R, S — Check spelling

Alt + Shift + S — Mark index entry

Alt + Control + F — Insert footnote

Alt + Control + D — Insert endnote

Additional Mac Shortcuts

COMMAND + N — New document

COMMAND + O — Open file

COMMAND + S — Save file

COMMAND + W — Close document

COMMAND + E — Center text

COMMAND + L — Left-align text

COMMAND + R — Right-align text

COMMAND + K — Insert link

COMMAND + Shift + E — Activate/deactivate tracking

OPTION + Left Arrow — Move cursor one word to the left

OPTION + Right Arrow — Move cursor one word to the right

OPTION + Up Arrow — Move cursor to the start of the previous paragraph

OPTION + Down Arrow — Move cursor to the start of the next paragraph

COMMAND + Home or *Command + Fn + Left Arrow* — Beginning of document

COMMAND + End or *Command + Fn + Right Arrow* — End of document

COMMAND + Delete — Delete one word to the left

COMMAND + Fn + Delete — Delete one word to the right

COMMAND + Enter — Insert page break

PAGE Up — Up one screen

PAGE Down — Down one screen

SHIFT + F3 or *Fn + Shift + F3* — Toggle case of selected text

COMMAND + Option + A — Insert comment

F7 or *Fn + F7* — Check spelling

COMMAND + Option + Shift + X — Mark index entry

COMMAND + Option + F — Insert footnote

COMMAND + Option + E — Insert endnote

Index

Notes

Notes